Emil and the Detectives

ERICH KÄSTNER

Level 3

Retold by Rod Smith
Series Editors: Andy Hopkins and Jocelyn Potter

Pearson Education Limited
Edinburgh Gate, Harlow,
Essex CM20 2JE, England
and Associated Companies throughout the world.

ISBN 0 582 42699 5

This edition first published 2000

NEW EDITION

Copyright © Penguin Books Ltd 2000
Illustrations by Madeleine Baker
Cover design by Bender Richardson White

Typeset by Pantek Arts Ltd, Maidstone, Kent
Set in 11/14pt Bembo
Printed in Denmark by Norhaven A/S, Viborg

Published by Pearson Education Limited in association with
Penguin Books Ltd, both companies being subsidiaries of Pearson Plc

For a complete list of the titles available in the Penguin Readers series please write to your local
Pearson Education office or to: Marketing Department, Penguin Longman Publishing,
5 Bentinck Street, London W1M 5RN.

Contents

Introduction

Emil went to the washroom at the end of the carriage. He took the little bag out of his pocket and counted the money. It was still there, but how could he make it safer? Then he remembered: there was a pin in his jacket. He took out the pin and pushed it through the bag, the paper money and the cloth of his inside pocket. The money was safe now.

Emil Fisher is travelling alone to his grandmother's house in the city. He is carrying money to her from his mother. But who are the other people on the train? Is his money really safe in the little bag in his pocket?

The writer of this story, Erich Kästner, was born in Dresden in Germany in 1899. He worked as a teacher, and then as a newspaper reporter. He became a full-time writer in 1927.

Emil and the Detectives came out in 1928 in German, and in English two years later. Then it was made into a film, and it was soon famous all over the world. The story was popular and successful because Erich Kästner was a good writer. He had a great sense of fun, but he also knew about children. He knew that they thought seriously about questions of right and wrong.

Kästner also produced other forms of literature. His poems, for example, were very important to him. They seemed amusing and they were easy to remember. But they had a serious message. Kästner saw the danger of the changes in Germany in the late 1920's and early 1930's. He attacked this danger in his funny, clever poems.

His attacks made the Nazis angry, and in 1933 they burnt his books. From 1933 to 1945, Kästner's writings were not printed in Germany. But he continued to write, and his work was printed in Switzerland.

After the war, Kästner was very busy. He continued with his writing, but he was also the president of PEN – an international writers' organization – from 1952 to 1962. He died in Munich in 1974.

Children love *Emil and the Detectives*. It is an exciting story, and Emil and his detectives are all children. But it is not just a children's book; it continues to be popular with older readers too.

Kästner describes people's actions and speech very well. Each person is very different from the others. So the reader can picture and hear each person clearly. Grandmother, for example, always says things twice. The Captain has a very loud voice; his father is a soldier and gives loud orders. Paul carries a car horn. Everyone knows him because of his horn.

The people in Kästner's book are like people that we know. 'Yes,' we think, 'that person behaves like my friend, or like someone in my family.' When Emil's mother prepares him for his first visit to the city, she is like a real mother. And then there is Emil. He is a good boy, and a brave one. He is real to us because he behaves like other clever little boys.

Kästner watched and understood children. When Polly is waiting for Emil at the station, she is very excited. But she is excited because she is proud of her new bicycle. She wants to show it to him. And she wants him to want one too.

The writer is not Polly or a child of her age. He is an adult, describing Polly. He describes her in an amusing way, so older readers like her too. Kästner's description of Little Tuesday is similar. The child doesn't only want to be a detective. He wants to be a police dog, because he can make the right noises.

Adults like the children's enjoyment of their adventure. For younger readers the adventure is more enjoyable than the people in it. They have the adventure with the children in the story, while older people watch it in their imaginations. Adults remember *their* adventures, when they were children.

Chapter 1   Emil Goes to the City

'Now, Emil,' said his mother, 'get ready. Your clothes are on your bed. Get dressed, and then we'll have our dinner.'

'Yes, Mother.'

'Wait a minute. Have I forgotten anything? Your other clothes are in your case. There's some food for your journey. These flowers are for your aunt. I'll give you the money for your grandmother after dinner. No, that's all, I think.'

Emil left the room and Mrs Fisher turned to her neighbour, Mrs Martin. 'My son's going to the city for two or three weeks. At first he didn't want to go. But what can he do here while his school's closed? My sister's asked us again and again to visit her. I can't go, because I have so much work. Emil's never travelled alone before, but he's old enough now. He'll be all right: his grandmother's going to meet him at the station.'

'I think he'll enjoy the city,' said Mrs Martin. 'All boys like it. There are so many things to see. I must go now, Mrs Fisher. Goodbye.'

Emil came back into the room and sat down at the table. His hair was tidy and he was wearing his best jacket. While he ate, he watched his mother. 'I mustn't eat too much,' he thought. 'She won't like it when I'm going away for the first time.'

But his mother was thinking about other things. 'Don't forget to write to me when you arrive,' she said.

'All right.'

'Give my love to your aunt and your grandmother and your cousin Polly. Look after yourself. And be good. I don't want anyone to say that you're not a polite boy.'

'I promise.'

After dinner Emil's mother went to the sitting-room. There

1

was a tin box on one of the shelves. She took out some money and came back to the table.

'Here's seventy pounds,' she said. 'Five ten-pound notes and four five-pound notes. Give your grandmother sixty pounds. I couldn't send the money to her before. But I've worked hard and I've saved it for her. The other ten pounds is for you. Your return journey will cost about three pounds. Use the other seven pounds when you go out. I'll put the money in this little bag. Now don't lose it! Where will you put it?'

Emil thought for a minute, then he put the bag into the pocket inside his jacket.

'It'll be safe there,' he said.

His mother looked serious. 'You mustn't tell anyone on the train about the money.'

'Of course not,' said Emil.

Some people think that seventy pounds is not a large amount of money. But it was a lot of money to Emil and his mother. Emil's father was dead, so his mother worked hard all day. She paid for their food and clothes, and for her son's books and his school. Emil realized that his mother worked hard. So he really tried to do well in class. She was always pleased when he got a good report from his teacher at the end of the year.

'Let's go now,' said Mrs Fisher. 'You mustn't miss the train. If the bus comes along, we'll take it.'

The country bus was very old and slow. Emil and his friends wanted modern buses in Newton. But other people in the town liked their old bus. They liked the driver, too. He always stopped at your house for you. You called out, and the driver stopped. But it was often quicker to walk.

The bus came and Emil and his mother got on.

They got off at the square in front of the station. Then they heard a deep voice behind them: 'Where are *you* going?'

It was Newton's chief of police.

Emil's mother said: 'My son's going to visit his grandmother for two or three weeks.'

Emil felt silly. He was remembering something.

In the centre of the station square there was a statue of a very famous judge. One day, after school, Emil and his friends climbed up and put an old cap on the statue's head. Then Emil began to paint its nose red. Suddenly, the chief of police walked into the square. 'Oh no, he saw me,' thought Emil, as he and his friends ran away.

Now, a week later, Emil waited for the policeman to say: 'Emil Fisher, come with me. You are going to prison.'

But the policeman didn't say anything as Emil carried his case into the station. Perhaps he was waiting until Emil came back from the city.

◆

Mrs Fisher bought a ticket for Emil. They only had to wait a few minutes for the train.

'Don't leave anything on the train. And don't sit on the flowers. Someone will lift your case up for you. Don't forget to say "please".'

'I can lift the case up,' said Emil. 'I'm not a baby.'

'All right.' His mother was looking serious again. 'You must get out at the right station in the city,' she said. 'It's the East Station, not the West Station. Your grandmother will be by the ticket office.'

'I'll find her, Mother.'

'Don't throw paper on the floor of the carriage when you eat your food. And don't lose the money.'

Emil opened his jacket and felt in his pocket.

'Don't worry,' he said. 'It's safe.'

The train came into the station. Emil kissed his mother and climbed into a carriage with his case. His mother gave him the flowers and food.

'Is there a seat for you?' she asked.

'Yes,' said Emil.

'Be good. And write to me.'

'You must write to me, too.'

'Of course. Now, be nice to your cousin, Polly.'

The carriage doors were shut and the train moved slowly out of the station.

Mrs Fisher waved her hand for a long time. Then she turned round and went home. She felt sad, but she only cried for a short time. She had to do her work.

Chapter 2   The Thief

Emil took off his school cap and said 'good afternoon' to the other people in the carriage.

He sat opposite a fat lady. She was only wearing one shoe, because her left shoe hurt her foot. She was sitting beside a man with a big nose.

'Boys are not usually so polite,' she said to the man.

As she talked, she moved her painful foot up and down.

Emil put his hand in his pocket. He wasn't happy until he felt the little bag. He looked at the other people in the carriage. They didn't look like thieves. There was another woman sitting to the right of the man with the big nose. She was sewing, making a cap for a baby. At the window, next to Emil, a man with a black hat was reading a newspaper.

Suddenly the man put down his paper and took some sweets from his pocket.

'Would you like one?' he asked Emil.

'Thank you very much,' said Emil, taking one of the sweets. 'My name's Emil Fisher,' he said.

The other people in the carriage smiled in a friendly way. The man lifted his hat and said: 'My name's Green.'

Then the fat lady asked Emil: 'Does Mr Smith still own the cloth shop in Newton?'

'Oh yes,' said Emil. 'Do you know him?'

'Yes. I'm Mrs James from Greenfield. I hope he's well. Can you tell him that?'

'Yes, of course,' replied Emil.

'Are you going to the city?' Mr Green asked Emil.

'Yes. My grandmother's meeting me at the East Station ticket office.' He felt in his pocket. The paper money in the bag made a little noise. It was still there.

'Do you know the city?'

'No.'

Emil looked at the other people in the carriage.

'Well, it will surprise you. Some of the houses there are 600 metres high. They tie the roofs to the sky. Then the houses don't move in the wind. And what do you do if you want to get to another part of the city quickly? Do you know?'

'No,' Emil answered, thinking, 'This is a strange man!'

'You're put in a box at the post office, and then you travel by post. And if you have no money, you can get fifty pounds from a bank. But you have to leave your head there ...'

'Is *your* head at the bank?' the man with the big nose said. 'Stop telling the boy stupid stories.'

The two men began to shout. Fat Mrs James stopped moving her foot, and the other woman stopped sewing.

Emil was happy, because the strange man couldn't talk to him now. He took out his food and began to eat his bread and butter. Then the train stopped at a big station. The two ladies and the man with the big nose got out. Mrs James was almost too late because she couldn't get her shoe on.

'Tell Mr Smith what I said,' she called to Emil as she left the train.

Now Emil and the man with the black hat were alone. Emil wasn't very pleased about this. He didn't want to be with a strange man who gave away sweets. A man who told silly stories. Emil wanted to feel the money again, but not in front of the other man. Then the train started again. Emil went to the washroom at the end of the carriage. He took the little bag out of his pocket and counted the money. It was still there, but how could he make it safer? Then he remembered: there was a pin in his jacket. He took out the pin and pushed it through the bag, the paper money and the cloth of his inside pocket. The money was safe now.

Emil went back to the carriage. Mr Green was asleep. Emil was glad – now he didn't have to talk to him. He looked out of the window. He enjoyed watching the trees, the fields and the houses.

Mr Green continued sleeping. Sometimes he made little

noises. Emil watched him. Why did he always keep his hat on? Emil noticed his long face and thin ears.

Suddenly Emil jumped with surprise. 'I nearly went to sleep. I mustn't do that,' he told himself. He didn't like being alone with Mr Green. Emil wanted more people in the carriage, but nobody came. He kicked his foot to stay awake. He sometimes did this at school in history lessons.

For a short time, this helped him. He thought about his cousin, Polly. What did she look like now? It was two years since he last saw her. He couldn't remember her face very well.

Some minutes later, he nearly fell off his seat. 'Have I been asleep?' he thought. He kicked his foot again. Then he counted the flies on the window. He counted them from the bottom to the top, he counted them from the top to the bottom, and then he counted them again. First there were twenty-four, then there were twenty-three. 'Why does the number change?' Emil asked himself. Then he fell asleep.

◆

When Emil woke up, he was lying on the floor of the carriage. The train was moving. He remembered his dream. It was a bad dream. The policeman from Newton was running after him. He caught him and took him to the stone judge. The judge was alive and said: 'Emil Fisher, you painted my nose, so you must go to prison.'

Slowly Emil began to remember. Of course, he was going to the city. Did he fall asleep, like the man in the black hat ...?

But the man wasn't there. Emil was alone in the carriage. He sat up. His knees were shaking. He got up from the floor. His clothes were dirty, so he cleaned them quickly with his hands. Then he felt in his inside pocket.

The money wasn't there!

Emil felt a sharp pain and pulled his hand from his pocket. There was blood on his finger from the pin, but there was no little bag there.

Emil began to cry.

Of course, he was not crying about the blood. He was crying about the money. His mother worked so hard, and now there was no money for his grandmother or for his visit to the city.

'I've been careless, and a thief has stolen my money. Now what can I do?' he thought. 'How can I get off the train and say to my grandmother: "Here I am, but I have no money for you. And you must give me the money for my ticket back to Newton." I can't stay in the city. I can't go home again.'

There was an alarm above the window at one end of the carriage.

Emil thought, 'If I ring the alarm, the train will stop. A railway guard will come to the carriage. He'll ask: "What's happened? What's the matter?" And I'll say: "Someone's stolen my money." "Why didn't you look after it?" he'll answer. "What's your name? Where do you live? You stopped the train. Now your family will have to pay twenty-five pounds."'

In fast trains there is a corridor that you can walk along. It takes you to the place where the guard sits. Then you can report a crime. But Emil was in a slow train. There is no corridor on slow trains. You must wait until the train stops at the next station.

'What's the time?' Emil thought. The train began to pass large houses with bright gardens, and tall buildings with dirty windows. The train was moving more slowly now.

Emil knew what to do. 'At the next station I must call the railway guard and tell him everything. The railway company will tell the police. But then I'll have problems with the police,' he thought, remembering his dream. 'They'll ask the Newton police about me.' He imagined the Newton police chief's report:

Emil Fisher of Newton is not a good boy. He paints the noses of statues. I do not believe that his money was stolen. Perhaps he was careless and lost it. But he probably hid it because he wanted to use it for himself. Emil Fisher is the thief. We must put him in prison.

Emil thought about the report and was afraid. No, he couldn't tell the police.

He took his case down and put on his cap. Then he put the pin back in his jacket and got ready.

The train stopped. Emil looked out of the window and saw a sign on a wall. It said: WEST STATION. The doors were opened and people got out of the carriages. Friends were waiting to meet them.

Suddenly he saw a black hat in the crowd. It was some metres away. Was it the thief? Perhaps he stole Emil's money but didn't leave the train. Perhaps he just moved to another carriage while the train was at one of the stations.

Emil got out quickly.

Then he remembered the flowers. He put down his case and jumped back into the carriage. He got out again with the flowers and picked up his case. Then he ran as fast as he could towards the gate.

Where was the black hat? There it was. Or was it a different hat? Emil's case was heavy. He wanted to put it down and leave it. 'But someone will steal it,' he thought.

At last he got through the crowd. He was now closer to the black hat.

Was it the thief? No.

There was another one. No, that man was too short.

Emil ran in and out of the crowd.

There! There was Mr Green, the thief. He was passing through the gate and he seemed to be in a great hurry.

'I'll get you!' thought Emil angrily.

He gave his ticket to the railway man, put his case in his other hand and, with the flowers under his right arm, ran after the black hat.

'It's now or never!' he thought.

Chapter 3   Emil Goes After the Thief

Emil wanted to run after the man and shout: 'Give me my money!'

'But,' he thought, 'the man won't say: "Of course, dear boy. Here it is. I promise that I'll never steal again."'

No, now he could only watch the man.

A very fat lady was walking in front of Emil. He hid behind her and followed the thief out of the station.

'If I ask that lady for help,' Emil thought, 'she probably won't believe me.'

The man walked into the station square. He crossed the road. An electric tram with two carriages turned into the road from the right. The man got into the first carriage and sat down next to a window.

Emil ran after the tram. The tram started moving as he reached the second carriage. He jumped on the tram, put his case in a corner and stood in front of it.

Cars hurried past the tram. There was a lot of noise, and there were a lot of people. There were newspaper boys at every corner, and wonderful windows filled with books, gold watches, shoes and food. And the buildings were very, very high.

'So this is the city!' Emil thought.

He wanted to look at everything, but there was no time. 'The man with my money will get off the tram and escape into the crowd. Then everything will be hopeless,' he thought.

Emil thought about his grandmother. She was waiting for him at the ticket office in East Station.

The tram stopped. Emil watched the carriage in front. A crowd of new passengers got on, but nobody got off. One man was angry because he fell over Emil's case.

A man inside the tram was selling tickets. He rang the bell and the tram moved again.

Suddenly Emil thought: 'Oh, no. I haven't got any money. If I can't pay for the ticket, I'll have to get off.'

'So this is the city!' Emil thought.

He looked at the other passengers. 'Can I say to one of them: "Please give me some money for my ticket"?' he thought.

One man was reading a newspaper. Two others were talking about a bank robbery.

'The thieves made a hole underground,' one of them was saying, 'and they went through the hole into the bank. They stole thousands of pounds.'

The other man laughed. 'Who can believe what people say?' he asked. 'Perhaps only a little money was taken.'

'No,' thought Emil. 'They won't believe *me*.'

The ticket man came nearer and nearer to Emil.

'Tickets! Tickets, please!' he called out.

People gave him their money and received their tickets.

He reached Emil. 'And you?' he asked.

'I've lost my money, sir,' Emil said.

'Lost your money? I've heard that story before. And where do you want to go?'

'I ... I ... don't know yet,' said Emil.

'Well, then, get off at the next stop!'

'No, I can't do that. I must stay here. Please, sir.'

'If I tell you to get off, you get off. Do you understand?'

'Oh, give the boy a ticket!' said the man who was reading a newspaper. He gave the ticket man some money, and Emil received his ticket.

'A lot of boys tell me they've lost their money,' said the ticket man. 'Then they laugh at me behind my back.'

'This one won't laugh at you,' said the man with the newspaper.

'Thank you very much, sir,' Emil said.

'Oh, that's all right,' the man with the newspaper said.

'Excuse me, sir. Where do you live?'

'Why do you want to know?'

'I want to give you back your money. I'm staying here for

a few weeks, so I can bring it to you. My name's Emil Fisher, from Newton.'

'Oh, forget about it,' said the man.

The tram stopped again. Emil watched. Did the man in the black hat get off? He saw nothing.

The tram continued its journey. Emil looked at the beautiful wide roads. He had no idea where he was going. The thief was still sitting in the other carriage. Nobody seemed interested in Emil. Even the kind man was reading his newspaper again.

The city was so large and Emil felt so small. It didn't matter to anyone that he had no money. Two million people lived in the city, and nobody was interested in his problems.

'What's going to happen?' Emil thought. He felt very unhappy.

◆

Emil's grandmother and his cousin Polly were waiting for him at East Station. They were standing near the ticket office, looking at the time every minute. A lot of people passed them, carrying boxes, cases and flowers. But not one of them was Emil.

'Perhaps he passed us and we didn't see him,' said Polly. She stood on the platform with her shining new bicycle. She wanted to show it to Emil. 'He'll want one too, when he sees it,' she thought.

Polly's grandmother was worried. 'What *is* the matter? What *is* the matter? I think the train arrived a long time ago.'

They waited a few more minutes, then Polly went to ask about the train.

A man was standing at the gate, looking at people's tickets. 'Has the train from Newton arrived yet?' Polly asked him.

'Newton? Oh, yes,' said the man. 'That train arrived a long time ago.'

Polly went back to her grandmother and gave her the news.

'Oh dear. What's happened? What's happened?' the old lady said.

'I think he got out at the wrong station,' said Polly. 'Boys are so stupid.'

They waited for another five minutes.

'We can't stay here,' said Polly. 'The next train from Newton is in two hours. Let's go home now. I'll come back here on my bicycle and meet him.'

'I don't like it. I don't like it,' said the old lady. When she was worried about something, she always said things twice.

At home, Polly's father and mother didn't know what to do. Polly's father wanted to write to Emil's mother.

'No, don't do that,' said his wife. 'Perhaps he'll be on the next train.'

'I hope he will,' said Polly's grandmother. 'But I don't like it. I don't like it.'

'I don't like it either,' said Polly, shaking her head wisely.

Chapter 4   Emil's Friends Make a Plan

At last the man in the black hat got off the tram. Emil picked up his case and the flowers, thanked the man with the newspaper, and followed the thief.

The thief walked in front of the tram, crossed the road and continued on the other side. The tram moved away, and Emil saw the man go into a café.

'Now,' thought Emil, 'I must be very careful.'

There was a house at the corner of the road. He ran into the doorway. It was a good place to hide. From there, he could see the thief easily.

Mr Green was sitting close to the café window. He was looking very pleased with himself. He ordered some coffee.

Emil didn't know what to do. 'I can't stay here and watch the man. A policeman will come along and tell me to move,' he thought.

Suddenly a horn sounded just behind Emil. He jumped and turned round quickly. A boy stood there, laughing at him.

'Don't be afraid,' said the boy.

'Did you make that loud noise?' asked Emil.

'Of course,' said the boy. 'You're not from here, are you? Everyone here knows me and my horn. I always carry it with me.'

'No, I'm not from here,' said Emil. 'I'm from Newton. I've just come from the station.'

'Newton? From the country? Is that why you're wearing those silly clothes?'

'Don't talk like that, or I'll hit you,' said Emil angrily.

The other boy looked surprised.

'I don't want to fight,' he said. 'It's too hot. But I will if you want to.'

'I haven't got time to fight now,' said Emil. 'I'm busy.'

'Busy? You aren't doing anything, just standing in this doorway.'

'Yes, I am,' Emil answered. 'I'm watching a thief.'

'What! Did you say "thief"?'

'That's right,' said Emil. He told the boy about losing all his money.

'Well, this is wonderful,' said the boy as Emil finished the story. 'It's like a detective film at the cinema. What are you going to do next?'

'I don't know.'

'Look. There's a policeman over there. Let's tell him. He'll help you.'

'I don't think so,' said Emil. 'I did something wrong in Newton. I think the police want to catch me.'

'Oh, I see,' said the boy. He thought for a minute, then said: 'I'll help you, if you want me to.'

'I'd like that,' said Emil.

'My name's Paul,' said the boy.

'And mine's Emil.'

'Well, Emil,' said Paul. 'We must do something. Have you got any money now?'

'Not a penny.'

Paul sounded his horn softly. It usually helped him think. But it didn't help this time.

'Can you bring some of your friends here?' asked Emil.

'Good idea,' said Paul. 'I'll run round to their houses and sound my horn. Then they'll come out and help us.'

'OK, but come back soon,' said Emil. 'If the thief leaves, I'll have to follow him. Then you won't know where I am.'

'That's true. But I don't think the man will leave yet. He's eating some eggs.'

Paul ran off.

Emil felt much happier. Friends are a great help when you are in trouble.

Emil watched the thief. He was enjoying his meal. Perhaps he was paying for the food with Mrs Fisher's money. But things were different now. Emil had help at last.

Ten minutes later, Emil heard the horn again. He saw about twenty boys coming up the road towards him.

Paul was in front. 'What do you think of this?' he asked Emil.

'Great,' said Emil, looking at all the boys.

'I've told them what happened,' Paul continued. He turned to the other boys. 'This is Emil. And the man who stole his money is sitting in that café. He mustn't escape.'

'We'll soon catch him,' said a boy with a loud voice.

'This is the Captain,' Paul said. He then told Emil the names of all the other boys.

'Well,' said the Captain wisely, 'we must begin. First, everyone must give me their money.'

Each boy threw his money into Emil's cap. A very small boy called Little Tuesday put five pence into the cap. He was very excited because it was his job to count the money.

'We have eighty-five pence,' Little Tuesday reported. 'Three of us will keep the money. If we can't stay together, there'll always be someone with money.'

'Good idea,' said the Captain. He and Emil each kept twenty pence. Paul took the rest.

Emil thanked everyone and said: 'I'll return the money after we catch the thief. But I can't do much with this case and these flowers. I'd like to leave them somewhere safe.'

'Give them to me,' said Paul. 'I know the man who owns that café. I'll leave them with him. And I'll have a good look at the thief while I'm there.'

'Be careful,' said the Captain. 'We don't want the thief to know you're watching him.'

When Paul came back, Emil said: 'Now I think we should have a meeting. But not here. Everyone can see us.'

Each boy threw his money into Emil's cap.

'We'll go over to the square and sit on the grass,' said the Captain. 'But some boys must stay here and watch the thief. They can be the "watchers" – two can watch the café and five or six others can stand along the road. If anything happens, they can run to the square. Then we'll come back here.'

'I'll choose the watchers,' Paul said to Emil and the Captain. 'And I'll stay here too and watch the café. You take the rest of the boys with you. Hurry. It's getting late now.'

Paul chose the boys that he needed. The rest went to the square with Emil and the Captain.

◆

They sat down on two long seats in the middle of the square by the grass. They all looked very serious. Then the Captain began to speak in a loud voice. His father was a soldier and always spoke like that when he gave orders.

'It's possible,' the Captain said, 'that later we won't be able to stay together. If that happens, we'll need a telephone. Who has a telephone at home that they can use?'

'I have,' Little Tuesday called out. 'My family's out at the cinema tonight.'

'And what's your telephone number?' the Captain asked.

'West 5478.'

The Captain thought for a minute. He turned to a boy named John.

'Take this pencil and paper. Cut the paper into twenty pieces. Write Little Tuesday's telephone number clearly on each piece. Then give everyone a piece of paper with the number on it. Little Tuesday's house can be our telephone office. Our detectives must telephone that office when anything new happens. And when we want to know the news, we can telephone that number, too.'

'But I'm not at home,' said Little Tuesday.

21

'No, but you will be,' the Captain answered. 'Listen to me. We'll finish talking, and then you'll go home and sit by the telephone. It's very important work.'

John gave out the pieces of paper. Each boy put his piece carefully in his pocket.

The Captain continued: 'Some of you must follow the thief. But the others must stay here in the square. Then we'll know where you are. We'll find you if we need you. You can go home now. Tell your families that you'll be very late tonight. But one after the other, not all at the same time. John, you can go home with Little Tuesday. Run back here when there's something to report. I think that's all, isn't it?'

'We'll need something to eat,' said Emil.

Five boys ran off to get some food.

'I think you're all being silly,' said a boy called Peter. 'You're talking about food and telephones. But we need to talk about catching this thief. How are we going to catch him?'

'Can we get his fingerprints?' said a boy who read a lot of detective stories.

'Of course not!' said John. 'We can only hope to get back the money that he's stolen.'

'But if we steal the money from him,' said the Captain, 'we'll be thieves too.'

'That's right,' said Emil. 'It's wrong to take something from someone if he doesn't know about it.'

'OK, we've talked enough,' said the Captain. 'Now let's do something. We don't know yet how we're going to catch this man. But one thing's sure: he must give back the money.'

'I didn't understand what you said about stealing,' said Little Tuesday. 'How can I steal something that belongs to me? I own it, even if it is in another person's pocket.'

'You're too young,' said the Captain. 'You can't understand.'

'Are you sure we can all be good detectives?' asked Peter. 'We don't want the thief to know what's happening. He'll escape.'

'Yes, we'll need some good detectives,' cried Little Tuesday. 'That's why you need me! I can be a wonderful police dog, too. I can make a noise like a dog.'

Nobody listened to him.

'Perhaps the thief has a gun,' said Peter.

'Then we need brave detectives,' said Emil. 'If anyone's afraid, they can go home to bed.'

Nobody moved.

'There's one more thing,' Emil continued. 'I must send news to my grandmother. She doesn't know where I am. She'll go to the police, and we don't want that. Can someone take a letter to 15 Bridge Street for me?'

'I'll do it,' said a boy called Robert.

Emil asked for a pencil and paper. He wrote:

Dear Grandmother,

You probably want to know where I am. Please don't worry. I am in the city. I cannot see you yet because I have some important business. But when everything is finished, I will come. Do not ask what this business is. The boy who is bringing you this letter is a friend. He knows where I am. But he cannot tell you because it is a secret. Give my love to Uncle, Aunt and Polly.

Your loving grandson,
Emil

Emil wrote the number of the house and the name of the street on the other side of the paper. Robert took it. The Captain gave him the money for his tram ticket, and Robert hurried away.

The five boys came back with the food. Emil gave some food to each of the detectives. Some of the boys were still at home. Their families did not want them to come out again.

23

The Captain then gave them all a secret word. The word was 'Emil', because it was easy to remember. When they phoned Little Tuesday, they had to say this word first. If a caller knew the word, they were a friend.

The Captain turned to Little Tuesday: 'Please telephone my father. Tell him that I have some important business. I won't be home until late.'

'All right,' said Little Tuesday. He went home, taking John with him.

'Won't your father be angry?' asked Emil in surprise.

'My father knows I'm sensible,' answered the Captain. 'I've promised him that I'll never do anything wrong. I can do what I like. But I mustn't break that promise.'

'Why aren't all fathers like that?' said Peter.

The Captain turned to the rest of the boys. 'I'll leave my money here,' he said. 'We have enough without it. Gerald, you must be the chief. Wait here until we send for you. John will come from Little Tuesday's house if we need help. Are there any more questions? Is everything clear? Our secret word is "Emil". Don't forget.'

'Secret word: "Emil",' the boys cried loudly. All the people in the square looked at them with surprise.

Emil was really enjoying himself now. 'I'm almost glad that thief stole my money,' he thought.

Chapter 5   Following the Thief

Three of the watchers ran into the square waving their arms. This was the sign. Mr Green was leaving the café!

'Let's go!' the Captain cried, and he, Emil and three other boys ran back to Paul. He was waiting for them in the doorway of the house.

The thief was standing outside the café, buying a newspaper. He opened the newspaper and began to read.

'He's looking over the top of the newspaper. He wants to see if anyone's watching him,' said Emil.

'I watched him very carefully,' said Paul, 'and he didn't look at me once. He just continued eating.'

The thief put the newspaper in his pocket and looked around him. A taxi came past. He shouted and it stopped. He got in, shut the door, and the taxi drove away.

The boys got into another taxi.

'Follow that taxi,' Paul said to the driver. 'Follow it carefully, please. The man inside mustn't see us. We're following him.'

'What's the matter?' the taxi driver asked.

'It's a secret,' Paul said. 'The man's done something wrong.'

'All right, but have you got any money?'

'Of course!'

They drove through the streets. A few people looked surprised when they saw so many boys in one taxi.

'Down! Down!' Paul said in a low voice. The boys threw themselves on the floor of the taxi.

'What's the matter?' asked the Captain.

'The traffic lights are red. We can't move until they change. The other taxi's stopped too, and we're just behind it. If the man turns round, he'll see us.'

The driver looked round at the boys and began to laugh. Then the lights changed to green. The boys got off the floor and sat in their seats again.

'I hope this isn't going to be a long journey,' said the Captain. He was thinking about the money.

But soon the first taxi stopped in a square at the door of a hotel. The thief got out, paid the driver and went into the hotel.

'Follow him, Paul,' said the Captain. 'If the hotel has another door, he'll escape.'

Paul ran after the thief and the other boys got out of the taxi. Emil paid the driver. Then they followed the Captain through a gateway and into a large courtyard behind a cinema. The Captain sent a boy called Tony after Paul.

'I hope the thief stays in that hotel,' Emil said. 'We can watch him easily from here. This courtyard is a wonderful place for our head office.'

'Yes, and it's near the trams and the post office telephones, too,' the Captain agreed.

He sat on a seat in the courtyard. He looked very serious, like someone who was planning a war.

Paul came back.

'The thief took a room in the hotel,' he said, excitedly. 'And there's only one way out. I checked. We've got him.'

'Is Tony watching the hotel?' the Captain asked.

'Of course.'

The Captain gave a boy called Walter some money. 'Phone Little Tuesday,' he said.

Walter ran to the post office.

'Is that you, Tuesday?'

'Speaking,' Little Tuesday replied.

'Secret word: "Emil". Walter speaking. The thief is staying at the West End Hotel, Princess Square. Our head office is in the courtyard behind the West End Cinema.'

Little Tuesday wrote everything down very carefully, and then Walter told him about the taxi journey.

'Why can't I be there with you?' Little Tuesday said. He felt sad and lonely, sitting by the telephone.

'Have any of the others phoned you?'

'No.'

'OK. Goodbye, for now.'

Walter went back to the courtyard. It was getting late.

'I'm sure we won't catch him today,' said Paul.

The boys thought deeply for some time. The sky was growing dark. They weren't sure what to do next.

Suddenly they heard a bell. It was coming nearer. A shining new bicycle came into the courtyard. A girl was riding it, and behind her was Robert.

Emil jumped up and said: 'That's my cousin, Polly.'

The Captain offered Polly his seat and she sat down.

'Well, Emil,' Polly began. 'We were just going to the station to meet the next train from Newton. Then your friend Robert arrived with the letter. You have some very nice friends.'

Robert looked pleased.

'And now,' Polly continued, 'Father and Mother and Grandmother are probably asking where I am. I didn't tell them anything. I just left the house with Robert. We phoned your office and spoke to Little Tuesday. And so here we are. But I must go back home now.'

'Were the family angry with me?' asked Emil.

'No. Grandmother just talked and talked until Father and Mother told her to be quiet.' Polly stood up. 'I hope you catch your thief tomorrow. Who's your chief detective?'

'This boy,' said Emil. 'He's the Captain.'

'I'm pleased to meet a real detective,' said Polly.

The Captain looked proud of himself.

'And now I must go,' Polly said. 'I'll come back in the morning. Goodbye.'

Polly rang the bell on her bicycle and rode away.

◆

Time passed slowly.

Emil went to see Walter and Tony, the two boys who were guarding the hotel. Then he went to the hotel, looked in and went back to the courtyard.

'We can't go home,' he said. 'Someone should stay and watch for us. There's a boy in the hotel who works in the lift. Let's speak to him. Perhaps he'll help us.'

'That's a good idea,' said the Captain. 'You're not as silly as most people from the country.'

'City people don't know everything,' Emil replied. He felt a little angry.

The other boys didn't want the thief to see Emil. So Paul went to speak to the lift boy.

Emil and the Captain went out of the courtyard. They stood by the gateway eating bread and butter.

It was nearly night time. Electric lights shone everywhere. The noise of trams, bicycles and taxis seemed even louder now. There was dance music coming from the West End Hotel. Crowds of people were going into the cinema.

'The city is wonderful, of course,' Emil said, 'but I wouldn't like to live here all the time. Newton is much smaller, but it's big enough for me. There's too much noise here.'

'I like the city,' said the Captain. 'And if you live here, you don't notice the noise.'

About an hour later, Peter and a number of other boys came into the courtyard. They were carrying a lot of food.

The Captain was very angry. 'What are you doing here?' he shouted. 'I told you to stay in the square.'

'Don't shout,' said Peter. 'We want to know what's happening here.'

'John didn't come from Little Tuesday's house with any news,' said Gerald. 'So we thought something was wrong. That's why we came.'

'How many boys are in the square?' asked the Captain.

'Three or four,' said one of the boys.

'No, I think there are only two,' said another.

'That's enough!' shouted the Captain. 'Is there *anyone* in the square?'

'Stop shouting,' said Peter. 'You can't tell us what to do.'

'I don't think you should be a detective,' said the Captain. 'We don't want you.'

Peter said some rude words and went away.

A boy came through the gateway. He was dressed in green and there was a green cap on his head.

'Is that the lift boy?' asked the Captain. Nobody answered.

The boy came towards them. Suddenly a horn sounded and the boy in green began to laugh. It was Paul.

'Don't you know me?' he asked.

Everyone laughed. A window above the courtyard opened and someone shouted: 'Be quiet down there!'

The Captain looked serious. 'We mustn't make a noise,' he said. 'Come here, Paul. Why are you dressed like that?'

'Well, I went to the hotel,' Paul began, 'and the lift boy was standing by the lift. I waved and he came over to me. I told him everything about Emil and the thief. He wanted to help, so he gave me some of his clothes. "People will think you're another lift boy," he said. "You can watch the thief. He won't know who you really are." And that's why I'm wearing these clothes.'

'But what about the hotel doorman?' Emil asked.

'The lift boy told him about us,' replied Paul. 'The hotel doorman is the lift boy's father. So it's OK. Now I can stay there all night. And I can take one of you with me, too. The thief is in room 61. I went up and stood near the door in these clothes and watched. After about half an hour, he came out and went to the toilet at the end of the corridor. When he came back, I stepped in front of him. "Is there anything I can do for you, sir?" I asked. "Oh yes," he said. "Tell them to call me at eight o'clock tomorrow morning. Don't forget." "Yes, sir," I said. Then he went back into his room.'

The Captain was very pleased and thanked Paul. Emil thanked him, too. Now everyone was very excited about the next day. They were all thinking the same thing: "Tomorrow we'll catch the thief."

'We can't do anything more tonight,' said the Captain. 'You can all go home to bed. But you must be back here early tomorrow morning. And try to bring some more money. I'll phone Little Tuesday now, and tell him to send the others home.'

'I'll go to the hotel with Paul,' Emil said.

Soon everyone was asleep. Most of the boys were in their beds at home, but not all of them. Paul and Emil were sleeping in a room at the West End Hotel, and Little Tuesday was asleep in his father's chair next to the telephone. He was dreaming of hundreds of telephone calls.

Some time later, Little Tuesday's father and mother came home. They were surprised to find him asleep in a chair.

His mother carried him up the stairs. 'Secret word: "Emil", secret word: "Emil",' Little Tuesday said in his sleep.

Of course, his mother didn't understand.

Chapter 6   The Thief is Caught!

Early next morning, the thief was dressing. He looked out of his window and noticed a large crowd of boys in the street below. Some of them were playing football in Princess Square. The others were standing there, talking.

'The schools are probably closed today,' he thought.

At the same time, the Captain was having a meeting in the courtyard at the back of the cinema. There were more boys than before and he was very angry again.

'I didn't want you to tell anyone about our plan,' he shouted. 'And what do you do? You bring a lot of boys that we don't know. Our plan was a secret. It isn't now.'

'Don't be angry, Captain,' said Gerald. 'We'll catch the thief.'

'You can send all these boys home,' said Walter. He was trying to help.

'No, I can't,' said the Captain. 'They won't go.'

'There's only one thing to do, then,' said Emil. 'We must change our plans. We can't follow the thief secretly now; there are too many boys. So he must see what we're doing. When he comes out of the hotel, we'll make a circle of boys around him. That circle will follow him everywhere he goes. He won't be able to escape.'

'Good idea!' said the Captain. 'I was thinking that, too.'

'The boys in the circle should make a lot of noise,' said Emil. 'Then other people will notice what's happening. The thief will want to give us the money back before the police arrive.'

There was the sound of a bell at the gateway. Everyone turned round. Polly rode into the courtyard.

'Good morning, detectives,' she said.

She jumped off her bicycle and took a bag from the front.

'I've brought you some coffee,' she said. 'And some food.'

The boys weren't really hungry. It was too soon after breakfast

31

to eat again. But they didn't want to be rude, so they took the bag. They ate and drank everything.

Suddenly they heard Paul's horn. He ran into the courtyard, shouting: 'Quick! Let's go! The thief's leaving the hotel.'

All the boys ran through the gateway. Polly was left alone with her bicycle and the empty bag. She wasn't very pleased. She jumped on her bicycle and rode after the boys. 'I don't like it! I don't like it!' she said. She sounded like her grandmother.

The thief came out of the hotel and turned to the right. The Captain sent Tony and Walter to the different groups of boys. They gave them their orders.

In three minutes there was a large crowd of boys all around the thief.

He didn't know what to do. The boys were talking, laughing and following him everywhere. 'And why are they looking at me all the time?' he thought. He couldn't understand what was happening.

Suddenly a ball flew past his head. He didn't like that and began to walk more quickly. But the boys walked faster, too.

He tried to turn into a side street, but another crowd of boys stood in his way.

'Walk in front of me,' Emil said to Paul. 'The thief mustn't see me yet.'

Polly rode at the side of the crowd, ringing her little bell.

The thief was feeling more and more nervous. He didn't know what he should do next. He tried walking faster, but he couldn't escape.

Suddenly he turned round and ran back along the street. The crowd followed. Then Walter ran in front of the thief and the man nearly fell.

'What's the matter with you?' Mr Green shouted. 'Go away, or I'll call a policeman.'

'Oh, yes please,' said Walter. 'That's what we're waiting for.'

Of course, the thief didn't want to call a policeman. He looked

In three minutes there was a large crowd of boys all around the thief.

up. People were looking at him from their windows. Was anyone phoning the police? 'If the police come,' he thought, 'they'll start asking questions.' He was beginning to feel afraid. He didn't know what to do.

Then he saw a bank across the road. It gave him an idea. He ran through the crowd of boys and hurried into the bank.

The boys followed. The Captain stopped them at the door and said: 'Paul and I will go inside. Emil can stay here until we're ready for him. When Paul sounds his horn, Emil and ten boys must come into the bank.' He turned to Emil: 'Bring some good boys, Emil. This will be a difficult business.'

Paul and the Captain walked into the bank. Mr Green was standing in front of a desk. Behind the desk, a bank assistant was having a telephone conversation.

The Captain got close to the thief. Paul stood behind him, with his hand in his pocket, ready to sound his horn.

The bank assistant finished telephoning and came to the desk.

'What can I do for you?' he asked Mr Green.

'Can you change these seventy pounds for me, please? I'd like five-pound notes for the ten-pound notes, and one-pound notes for the five-pound notes.' He took the money out of his pocket.

'Stop!' the Captain called out. 'That money was stolen.'

'What!' said the bank assistant in surprise.

The other people in the bank looked up from their work.

'This man stole that money from my friend,' said the Captain. 'But if he changes the money into smaller notes, nobody can prove it.'

'You crazy boy!' shouted Mr Green.

He hit the Captain in the face. The Captain hit him back, hard, in the stomach. All the bank workers ran to the desk to watch.

Paul sounded his horn.

Ten boys came running into the bank. Emil was in front. They all stood around Mr Green.

The bank manager came out of his office.

'What's all this noise about?' he asked.

Emil pointed to the thief. 'Yesterday afternoon, this man here stole my money. He took it while I was asleep on the train from Newton.'

'Can you prove this?' the manager asked.

Mr Green laughed. 'Of course he can't! I've been here for a week. Yesterday I was in the city all day.'

'That isn't true!' Emil shouted angrily. He was almost crying.

'Can you prove that this is the same man? The man who was on the train yesterday?' the manager asked.

Emil thought for a minute. His friends began to look worried.

'Yes, I can!' Emil said at last. 'There was a lady in the carriage for the first part of the journey. Her name is Mrs James and she lives in Greenfield. I remember, because she asked me to speak to her friend Mr Smith. He owns a cloth shop in Newton.'

The bank manager turned to the thief. 'And can you prove that you were in the city all day yesterday?' he asked.

'Of course I can,' the thief answered. 'I was at the West End Hotel in Princess Square. That's where I'm staying.'

'But only since yesterday evening,' Paul said. 'I know that for a fact. I've been there, dressed as a lift boy.'

The other bank workers smiled. They wanted to believe the boys' story. But the bank manager looked serious. 'I must keep this money for now,' he said.

He took a piece of paper and began to write down their names and addresses.

'The man's name is Green,' Emil said.

The thief laughed loudly. 'You can see that there's been a mistake. My name's Miller, not Green.'

'In the train yesterday, he called himself Green,' Emil said.

'Can you prove that your name's Miller?' asked the bank manager.

'I have no papers with me,' said the thief, 'but I can get them from the hotel.'

'Don't believe him!' Emil cried. 'It's my money and I must have it back. My mother asked me to take the money to my grandmother. She lives here, in Bridge Street.'

'Perhaps that's true,' said the manager. 'But I'll have to ask you again. Can you prove that the money is yours? Is your name written on the back of the notes? Did you write down their numbers?'

'Of course not,' said Emil. 'I didn't think that I could lose the money.'

'Were there any marks on the notes?'

'I don't think so.'

'Well, that's the end of it, then,' the thief said. 'Everything that I've told you is true. That money's mine. I never steal from children.'

'Wait a minute!' Emil cried. 'Now I remember. There *is* a mark on the notes: the mark of a pin. I wanted to be sure that the money stayed in my pocket. So I put a pin through the cloth of my pocket and through the bag with the money in it. If you look closely at the notes, you'll see the holes from the pin.'

The bank manager held the notes up against the light. Everyone watched in silence. The thief stepped back.

'The boy's right,' said the manager. 'There are holes in these notes.'

'And here's the pin that made the holes,' Emil said. He put the pin from his jacket on the desk. Then he held his finger up. 'And here's the place where I pricked myself.'

The thief turned and pushed through the crowd of boys. Some of them fell down. He ran through the door of the bank and disappeared.

'Catch him!' cried the bank manager.

Everyone ran to the door.

The thief was outside. There were about thirty boys round

him. Some of them held his legs, some of them held his arms and some of them held his coat. There was no escape for him now.

A policeman came running towards them. Polly was with him.

The bank manager said to the policeman: 'Take this man to the police station. He's stolen this boy's money.'

The policeman held the thief's arm. 'Right,' he said. 'You come along with me!'

The bank assistant took the money and the pin and went with them.

All the boys and Polly went too. They were a strange group. First there was the policeman and the assistant from the bank, with the thief between them. Then came all the boys. And finally, there was Polly on her shining new bicycle. She called to Emil: 'I'm going to ride home and tell the family.'

She rang her little bell, turned into a side street and rode away.

Chapter 7   Policemen and Reporters

At the police station, the policeman told his chief everything that he knew. Emil added more information. He also had to give his name, date and place of birth, and address. The police chief wrote everything down.

'And what's your name?' he asked the thief.

'John Turner,' the man answered.

When they heard this, Emil, Paul and the Captain laughed loudly. Even the bank assistant laughed.

'First his name's Green,' Paul said, 'then it's Miller. And now it's Turner. So what's his real name? Why don't you ask him?'

'Silence!' said the police chief.

Mr Green-Miller-Turner gave the date and place of his birth. He was staying at the West End Hotel. No, he couldn't prove who he was. He didn't have any papers with him.

'And where were you before you came here yesterday?' the police chief asked.

'In Greenfield.'

'That isn't true!' cried the Captain.

'Silence!' the police chief shouted. He turned to the thief. 'Mr Turner, did you steal seventy pounds from the schoolboy Emil Fisher of Newton yesterday?'

'Yes,' said the thief sadly. 'I don't know why I did it. The boy was asleep in the corner of the carriage. I saw the bag with the money in it fall out of his pocket. So I picked it up. I only wanted to see what was in the bag. But because I didn't have any money ...'

'This isn't true,' Emil said. 'The money didn't fall out of my pocket. There was a pin through it.'

'And he *did* have some money,' the Captain said. 'He paid for food and a taxi yesterday. And today all Emil's money was still in his pocket.'

'Silence!' the police chief said again. 'I didn't ask you to speak.' He wrote everything down.

'Can't I go, sir?' the thief asked. 'I made a mistake and I'm sorry. You know where I'm staying. I'm in the city on business and I'd like to finish it today.'

The police chief didn't listen to him. He phoned the main police station for a car to take the thief away.

'When can I get my money back?' Emil asked.

'I don't know. They'll tell you at the main police station. You must go there now and report to the chief detective.'

The police car arrived a few minutes later and took the thief away. The other boys were standing outside the police station.

Emil gave them the news. He asked them to telephone Little Tuesday with the news, too.

Finally, he said: 'Thank you, everyone, for all your help. Soon I'll be able to pay back the money that you lent me.'

The boys were happy to help, they said. They didn't want the money back.

◆

Only Emil, Paul and the Captain went to the main police station. A policeman took Emil to see the chief detective. The others waited outside his office.

The chief detective was a pleasant man. He listened to Emil's story and then gave him back the money.

'Look after it now,' he said.

'I will,' said Emil. 'I'm going to take it to my grandmother.'

'You and your detectives did a very good job,' said the chief.

'Thank you, sir,' said Emil. 'Can I ask a question?'

'Of course.'

'What will happen to the thief?'

'We'll take his photograph, and his fingerprints. Then we'll check on our list of criminals. We'll see if he's there.'

'List of criminals?'

'Yes. It's a book. We keep photographs of all the people who've been to prison. It also has the fingerprints of thieves that we're trying to catch. Perhaps your thief is one of the men that we're looking for.'

The telephone rang.

'Just a minute,' the chief said. He spoke into the telephone. 'Yes. Come up to my office.'

He turned to Emil. 'A few people are coming up to see you. They're reporters from the newspapers.'

'Oh. Are they going to write about me in the newspapers?'

'I think so.' The chief smiled. 'When a schoolboy catches a thief, he becomes famous.'

The door opened and four reporters came into the room. The chief detective shook hands with them and told the story of Emil and the thief. The four reporters wrote everything down carefully.

'This is a wonderful story,' one of the reporters said. 'A boy from the country becomes a detective!'

'He should join the police,' said another man.

'Why didn't you go to the police at the beginning and tell them everything?' asked a third reporter.

Emil suddenly felt afraid.

'Yes, why didn't you do that?' asked the chief detective.

'Because,' Emil began slowly, 'I painted a red nose on the statue in the station square at Newton. Do . . . Do I have to go to prison?'

The reporters and the chief detective all laughed.

'Of course not, Emil,' said the chief. 'We aren't going to send one of our best detectives to prison.'

'Oh, I'm very happy about that,' Emil said. He turned to one of the reporters. 'Don't you remember me?' he asked. 'We were on the same tram yesterday. You paid for my ticket because I had no money.'

'Of course,' said the reporter. 'And you asked me where I lived. You wanted to come and give me back the money.'

'Can I give it to you now?' said Emil, taking some money out of his pocket.

'Of course not,' said the reporter. 'I've got a better idea. Come with me and I'll show you the offices of our newspaper. But first we'll go and have some tea and cakes.'

'I'd like to go with you very much,' said Emil. 'But Paul and the Captain are waiting for me outside.'

'Then they must come too,' said the reporter.

But they had to wait a few more minutes. The other reporters wanted to ask some more questions. Emil told them everything that they wanted to know. They wrote it all down.

'Is this the first time that Mr Green has stolen anything?' one of them asked the chief detective.

'I don't think so,' he replied. 'Phone me in an hour. It's possible that I'll have a big surprise for you.'

◆

The reporter from the tram put Emil, Paul and the Captain into a taxi, and they all drove away for tea and cakes. Paul sounded his horn on the way.

In the café, the boys ate a lot of cakes and told the reporter about their exciting adventure. They told him about the meeting in the square and how they followed the taxi. They told him how Paul dressed as a lift boy, and about the fight in the bank.

'You are three of the finest boys that I've ever met,' the reporter said at the end.

They all felt very proud of themselves.

◆

After tea, the reporter took Emil to the newspaper office. It was a very large building. People were running in and out of rooms all

Emil tidied his hair and someone took his photograph.

the time. Everyone seemed very busy. The place was filled with the sound of people typing.

They went into a room where a young lady was sitting. The reporter walked up and down, telling her Emil's story. Emil watched as she typed it all.

Then the reporter telephoned the chief detective's office.

He listened for some time. 'Really? Is that true?' Emil heard him say. 'You don't want me to tell him? Thank you very much. It will be a wonderful story for the newspaper.'

The reporter turned to Emil and said: 'Come with me, quickly. We must take your photograph.'

'Why?' asked Emil in surprise.

The reporter smiled.

They went up in the lift and into a large room. Emil tidied his hair and someone took his photograph. Then the reporter took Emil down to the street. He called a taxi to take Emil home.

'Goodbye,' the reporter said. 'And don't forget to read the newspaper this afternoon. I think you'll be very surprised.'

Chapter 8 With Grandmother at Last!

On the way to Bridge Street, Emil asked the driver to stop at the café. His case and the flowers were still there. He took them, thanked the owner of the café and got back into the taxi.

At last they arrived at his grandmother's house. Emil rang the bell. The door opened and his grandmother was standing in front of him. She kissed him, pulled his hair and said: 'Emil, you wild boy! We've heard some very strange stories about you!'

Polly and her mother came running from the kitchen. They both looked very pleased.

'Did you get the money back?' Polly asked.

'Of course,' Emil answered. He took the notes from his pocket and gave his grandmother sixty pounds.

'Here's the money, Grandmother,' he said. 'It comes with Mother's love. She's sorry that she couldn't send any for the last three months. But business wasn't very good. Now she's sent you more than usual.'

'Thank you very much, my child,' the old woman answered.

She gave him back one of the pound notes and said: 'That's for you, because you're an excellent detective.'

Emil thanked his grandmother. Then he gave the flowers to his aunt. She took the paper off them, and Polly brought a pot of water from the kitchen. But it was too late. The flowers were dead.

'Oh dear. They look like dry grass,' said Polly.

'They were fresh when Mother gave them to me,' Emil said sadly. 'But I couldn't give them any water yesterday.'

'It doesn't matter,' his grandmother said. 'Now we must have our dinner. Uncle won't be home before this evening. Can you help me please, Polly?'

◆

After dinner, Emil wanted to ride Polly's shining new bicycle, so he and Polly went out into the street. His grandmother lay down to rest. His aunt made an apple cake. Her apple cakes were famous.

As Emil was riding along Bridge Street, a policeman came past. 'Do you know where Number 15 is?' he asked.

'Yes. Why? Has something happened?' Emil replied. He was thinking about the statue again.

'No, no,' said the policeman. 'Are you the schoolboy Emil Fisher?'

'Yes, sir.'

The policeman didn't say another word. He just walked to the house and rang the bell.

◆

Emil's aunt asked the policeman to sit down in the sitting-room. His grandmother woke up. She wanted to know what was happening, too. Emil and Polly stood near the table. They were all excited.

'I have some news for you,' the policeman began. 'Emil and his detectives followed a bank thief. The police have wanted to catch the man for a long time. We found his fingerprints in our list of criminals, so he had to tell us everything. And this time his story was true. Most of the money that he stole was in his hat and inside his coat. It was all in hundred-pound notes.'

'Really?' said Polly. She couldn't believe it.

The policeman continued: 'Two weeks ago, the bank promised a reward to the person who found the thief. And you caught the man,' he said, turning to Emil, 'so you'll receive the reward. The chief detective is very pleased.'

The policeman took some notes from his pocket and put them on the table.

'Fifty pounds,' he said.

Emil looked at the money. He was too surprised to speak.

His grandmother gave the policeman a cup of coffee and then he left. The old woman put her arm round Emil, saying: 'I can't believe it! I can't believe it!'

Emil still couldn't speak, but Polly could. She jumped up and down, shouting: 'Now we can invite all the boys here to tea.'

'Yes,' Emil said. 'But first we must invite Mother.'

Chapter 9   Emil's Mother Goes to the City

The next morning, Mrs Fisher's neighbour, Mrs Martin, rang her doorbell.

'How are you, Mrs Fisher?' she asked.

'I'm worried about my son,' Mrs Fisher replied. 'He hasn't written to me since he went to the city. I'm watching for the postman all the time.'

'Well now you can stop worrying, my dear,' said Mrs Martin. 'I came to tell you that he's fine. He sends his love.'

'Where is he? How do you know?'

'He's very well. He's also famous. He caught a thief and was given a reward of fifty pounds. You must go to the city on the next train.'

'But who told you all this?'

'Your sister's just phoned me. You must go and see them immediately.'

◆

Later that afternoon, Mrs Fisher had another surprise. She was sitting on the train and a man opposite her was reading a newspaper. Suddenly she saw something on the front page.

'That's my son!' she cried, pointing to a photograph of Emil.

The man put down the newspaper and looked up in surprise. 'Really?' he said. 'So you're Emil Fisher's mother. I'm sure you're very proud of him. Here, you can read the story.' And he gave her the newspaper.

"COUNTRY BOY ACTS AS DETECTIVE", she read. "100 CHILDREN FOLLOW A THIEF".

Then came Emil's story.

Mrs Fisher read every word carefully. When she finished, she felt very proud of her son. So she read the story again – seven times.

Mrs Fisher read every word carefully.

Emil was waiting for her at East Station.

'Isn't it wonderful?' he said. 'And do you know what I'm going to do? I'm going to buy a new coat for you, and a football for me.'

His mother smiled. 'That's very nice of you, dear. But I've got a better idea. We'll put most of the money in the bank and save it. When you're older, it will be very useful to you.'

'Well, OK,' said Emil. 'But you'll still have your coat. And now I'd like you to meet my friends.'

'Where are they?'

'At Grandmother's house. Aunt has made one of her apple cakes, and we've asked all the boys to a tea party. They're there now, making a lot of noise.'

◆

And it *was* noisy when they arrived. All Emil's new friends were there: Paul, the Captain, Gerald, Walter, Robert, Tony, John, Little Tuesday and the others. There weren't enough chairs for everyone.

Polly was running from one table to another with a big pot of tea. Everyone was eating apple cake. The old grandmother was laughing happily.

Emil's mother thanked the boys for helping her son.

Suddenly the old grandmother stood up.

'Now listen to me, boys,' she began.

There was silence.

'I'm not going to tell you how wonderful you are,' she said. 'It isn't a good idea to be too proud of yourselves. It's true that you caught a thief. But there's one boy here who wanted to follow Mr Green with the rest of you. He wanted to go after him in a taxi, and dress in a lift boy's clothes and watch him secretly. But he didn't. He did what you told him to do. He stayed at home by the telephone and helped in that way.'

Everyone looked at Little Tuesday.

'Yes, I'm talking about Little Tuesday,' the grandmother continued. 'He stayed by the telephone for two days. It was a boring job, but he did it well. Now let's all stand up and thank Little Tuesday.'

And that is exactly what everyone did.

◆

The party ended, and all the boys went home. But first they promised to meet again before Emil went back to Newton.

The family sat and talked about Emil's adventure.

'Well,' said Emil, 'I've learnt one lesson. You can't believe everything that strangers tell you.'

'And I've learnt something, too,' said his mother. 'It's not a good idea for boys to travel alone.'

Emil's grandmother didn't agree. 'You're wrong, dear,' she said. 'You're wrong.'

'Perhaps,' said Emil's mother. 'But isn't there a lesson that we can learn from this?'

The old lady smiled. 'Yes, there is,' she said. 'Life is difficult sometimes, but there are many kind people in the world.' She turned to Emil. 'And a true friend comes when you need help.'

ACTIVITIES

Chapters 1–3

Before you read

1 Look at the pictures in this book. Which people are the detectives? Which person is the criminal?

2 Find the words in *italics* in your dictionary. They are all in the story.

  a Which of the words below are words for:

  – parts of a train?

  – another vehicle?

  – things that make a noise?

  – a crime?

  – a group of people?

  alarm bell carriage corridor organization robbery tram

  b What can you do with:

  – a *cap*?

  – a *pin*?

  – a *statue*?

  c How do you *behave* when you are alone at home?

  d Do you enjoy *sewing*? Why (not)?

After you read

3 In which order are these introduced in the story? Number them.

  – a pin

  – a baby's cap

  – a bicycle

  – a black hat

  – a statue

  – some sweets

  – a little bag of money

  – a case

4 Discuss which of the things above is the most important? Why?

Chapters 4–6

Before you read

5 Look at these chapter titles:

Chapter 4   Emil's Friends Make a Plan

Chapter 5   Following the Thief

Chapter 6   The Thief is Caught!

What do you think is going to happen in these chapters?

6 Are these sentences true or false? Check the words in *italics* in your dictionary.

  a A *captain* is a person who sells caps.

  b A *courtyard* is a piece of ground which has buildings or walls around it.

  c A *fingerprint* is a photograph of a finger.

  d In the past, cars had *horns*.

  e The *manager* of a bank is the cleaner.

  f A *mark* is a German policeman.

  g If you *prick* your finger, blood comes out.

After you read

7 Who says this? Why? Who is he talking to?

'It's very important work.'

8 Two things go wrong with the Captain's plan. Each time, he is angry. What exactly goes wrong, and why is he angry?

Chapters 7–9

Before you read

9 What story do you think the thief will tell in the police station?

10 Guess the correct answer. Then check in your dictionary. A *reward* is:

  a a newspaper report about a terrible crime

  b something that you are given when you behave well

  c money that is stolen from a bank in a robbery

After you read

11 These people are all happy with Emil and the detectives, but for a different reason. Why are they pleased?

   a the chief detective

   b the newspaper reporter

   c Mrs Fisher

   d the bank manager

12 Act out this telephone conversation.

   Student A: You are Emil's aunt. Phone Mrs Martin, Mrs Fisher's neighbour. Explain what has happened. Say why Mrs Fisher must come to the city immediately.

   Student B: You are Mrs Martin, Mrs Fisher's neighbour. Answer the phone. Ask for more information. You will need to tell Mrs Fisher everything.

Writing

13 You are Mr Green. You are sitting in your room in the West End Hotel. You feel very pleased with yourself. You know nothing about Emil's detectives. Write a letter to a friend. Explain what you are going to do with the money from your robberies.

14 You are the newspaper reporter who paid for Emil's ticket on the tram. Write a newspaper report about Emil's adventures from the time that you gave him the money.

15 The chief detective says to one of the reporters: 'Phone me in an hour. It's possible that I'll have a big surprise for you.' It is now one hour later. Write the telephone conversation between the detective and the reporter.

16 You are the Captain. It is a month after the end of this story. You and the detectives have had another adventure. Write to Emil and tell him about it.